Learn How to ReWild

By Richard Godbehere

Your Six Step Fast Track to Nature Recovery and Reconnection on Your Patch

quick solutions for nature lovers to champion and unleash wildlife at home and on their land

while also…

- finding sanctuary from eco-anxiety, stress and depression

- leaving a legacy for your kids, and those who come after, making your mark on wildlife recovery

- helping support and enrich the lives of your local community

- starting a learning adventure to last a lifetime

- discovering your place in the natural world, and in turn, new purpose amongst the vast, global, pro-nature community

- having fun on the journey, with new found friends, mad experiences, plus a whole load of exciting destinations to add to your bucket list

Learn How to ReWild

By Richard Godbehere

1st edition 2024

Copyright © 2024 Richard Godbehere

All rights reserved.

No part of this publication may be reproduced, distributed, or transmitted in any form or by any means, including photocopying, recording, or other electronic or mechanical methods, or by any information storage and retrieval system without the prior written permission of the publisher, except in the case of very brief quotations embodied in critical reviews and certain other noncommercial uses permitted by copyright law.

Table of Contents

Table of Contents 6
Introduction 9
Step One - plants 12
   Trees, woods and scrub 12
      Tree planting 14
   Hedges 17
   Meadowlands 20
      Existing Seed Banks 21
      Sowing Seeds 22
   Some further important points for trees, hedges and meadows 24
   Soils 27
Step Two - animals 29
   Herbivores 29
   Predators 38
   Scavengers and decomposers 43
   Invertebrates 45
   Other roles 48
Step Three - water 52
   Drainage 52
   Existing rivers and lakes 54
   New scrapes and ponds 58
Step Four - connections 61
   Scale 61
   Cores, corridors and stepping stones 63

Relationships 69
　　Fences, barriers and boundaries 72
Step Five - chemicals 75
Step Six - people 80
　　Connectivity 80
　　Roles 82
Checklist 86
Glossary 93
　　Introduction 93
　　Step One - plants 95
　　Step Two - animals 100
　　Step Three - water 106
　　Step Four - connections 108
　　Step Five - chemicals 110
　　Step Six - people 113
Acknowledgements 115
And finally... 116

Well I'd never have got here without you my love;
I can never thank you enough Jane.
But it's your time now to pursue and enjoy your own dreams xx

Introduction

Hello and welcome to this guide on how to make your plot a nature hotspot.

This is for that vast majority of people, that when opening a new washing machine, reach straight for the Quick Start Guide. This is the definitive what-to-do guide to unleashing nature.

If you are after the huge manual that teaches you the background to nature recovery, rewilding as a technique, how it works, why it works, how to plan and monitor your project, and exactly how to implement each action - this isn't it. However, if you want that level of detail, trust me at A Call to ReWild we have you covered. Please just get in touch.

I have split this book into six essential sections of nature recovery. Each one stands alone, leading to enviable results. However, the parts fit together like a puzzle. Work through all six (in any order), and you will return nature to a state of self sustainability, where it needs little to no input from us to thrive.

Each section will feature many actions to elevate that aspect of nature. However, not all actions will apply to your land, so don't stress if you don't want to reintroduce sea eagles. And please factor in some common sense too. For example, you cannot ethically stick a herd of cattle in a small suburban garden. Equally, if you are fortunate enough to have the River Thames running through your field - no you can't dam it without permission.

Rather than splitting nature recovery into six areas to focus on, I could have directed people to garden, field or farm activities instead. And I'm sure some readers will be wondering why I haven't. Well firstly, many of the actions in this guide can apply to different scales, so would have to be repeated for example in both the garden and the field section. Secondly, and maybe more importantly, gardens can vary in size between a small window box, and a few acres with a paddock. Equally farms can be a 5 acre smallholding up to a 1000 acre moorland or ranchland estate. So while, for example, garden activities may apply to some gardens, field activities may apply to others.

I must also apologise to any of you that aren't British that this book is rather UK-centric. I admit ashamedly any reference to British fauna, flora, institutions or wild sites may pass under the radar. Please fear not. Whilst all the examples are of temperate landscapes, the theory is universal, and equally applicable to dry steppes, tundra and tropical forests. The relationship between plants, herbivores, predators and decomposers is the same the world over. Plus the impacts of connections, water and chemicals are just as significant in different biomes. The biggest differences will be the difficulty of adding water in arid areas, and hence of plants to thrive. In these areas you may have to reel in your expectations of "green" somewhat. However, that doesn't mean you can't create an exemplary example of an ecosystem from your part of the world, that can still work its magic on wildlife, you, and any other people with access to your scheme.

So, dive in, have fun, meet people, learn to see the little things in the natural world that open your eyes to a new perspective, connect with your community, build the perfect refuge from life's struggles, supporting your health and wellbeing, and leaving a gift for the world, knowing you did your bit to protect us, and nature, our planetary support system. And by the way, thank you.

Step One - plants

All the oxygen we breathe and all the carbon in living things is produced or fixed by plants. This is where it all begins. So plants are a tad important, because without them, bar a few bacteria, nothing else would be here, including us. They shore up our rivers, prevent floods, protect our coasts from storms, enrich our soils, help us graze our domestic animals, and themselves form over half of our diets too.

But those are just *our* benefits from plants, what we call ecosystem services. Let's not forget they form the cornerstone of almost every habitat, and because of the oxygen they produce and the nutrients they gather, they truly are the basis of life on Earth. So what better place to start than to unleash the jungle!

Trees, woods and scrub

Trees are excellent 3D habitat for birds, bats, other mammals, invertebrates, lichens, mosses and children. They are often long lived, and spend as long in old age, and rotting down, as they do in their prime.

When old they are often termed veteran trees, and commonly have holes, splits, hollowing, and even puddles in their structure - making them incredibly rich habitats in their own right. These old monuments are regularly flags to seed banks from our very oldest times. Therefore please protect veteran trees (and the next generation of trees that will become veterans) as they are likely to be the greatest resource for nature on site, and they are *irreplaceable*. Even if you plant more trees elsewhere to compensate, then wait for 100-200 years for them to mature, you still won't recreate the amazing seed bank and mycorrhizal network (the wood wide web) that lies beneath.

Trees usually grow largest when they have no competition for light, so you usually see giants in hedgerows, the middle of fields, parklands in old rural estates, even as remnants of times gone by in the middle of towns and cities.

Woodlands can be modern or ancient, broadleaf or conifer, planted or semi-natural. (There are no natural woods left in the UK, although some sites have escaped management more than others). Woods are vital habitat to birds and invertebrates, with most mammals spending some part of their life cycle in one.

As with all things in the natural world, the more variety a woodland has, in tree age, height, species, spacing and structure, the more species it will in turn attract. So a dark coniferous plantation lies at one end of the scale, whereas a mixture of broadleaf and coniferous trees, regenerating randomly, (read naturally), with open glades, and copses, will provide much richer habitat.

Scrub is composed of woody plants under 5m; blackthorn, hawthorn, buckthorn, dogwood, dog rose, some willows (like goat, grey or downy), elder, hazel are all good examples. They often form dense thickets loved by roosting or nesting birds for cover. Scrub is often dismissed as messy, but is a vital habitat for nightingales amongst others, and often protects the seedlings of canopy trees like oak and ash until they are deer proof.

Tree planting

The ideal way to increase tree cover is for the trees to regenerate naturally or colonise new areas through wind or animal seed dispersal.

So to a point this is one where you can leave nature to carry on by itself.
UNLESS:

1. The seed sources (parent trees) are too far away

2. There are too many deer or domestic herbivores particularly sheep, for seedlings to grow
3. You need the trees to reach maturity quickly

But here are some solutions to these issues:

1. Collect local seeds e.g. acorns, chestnuts etc and plant them out yourself
2. Protect the tree seeds or seedlings from herbivores
    a. Try surrounding seedlings or planted seeds with a robust mound of thorny hedge trimmings - hawthorn or blackthorn are ideal and will last a few years; rose and bramble are good but don't last as long. You could always plant some rose and bramble instead so they grow and last until shaded out by the growing trees
    b. Similar, but try dead hedging around the seedlings. The hedge will need to be both dense and high enough to prevent jumping to resist deer. It's a lot of effort so while you may do it around an area of new tree planting, you'd be mad to do it around each seedling.
    c. Then you have the more standard tree guards, but shop carefully, for some are better for voles and mice, others for deer. Also please make sure you plan their removal in a few years time

    so we're not stuck with a load more plastic in the environment.
  d. Deer/stock fencing - expensive but usually effective. Again there's no point unless it's a significant planting area that you are surrounding.
3. If you want some mature trees more quickly, maybe again because of deer numbers, or because you want to turn things around more quickly, or because you want the benefits of those trees sooner - such as strengthening slopes/riverbanks, shade, habitat creation, then you might be best planting trees.

Please don't forget to try to mix the planting with natural regeneration, or stagger the planting over several years where possible, so that you have a mix of ages and heights, (woodlands don't naturally all start growing on the same day, and reach the same height together). That way you get greater structural variation in the wooded area, to attract greater numbers of animal species.

Hedges

Hedgerows act as animal corridors through the landscape, they give shade, they stop croplands eroding, prevent the spread of chemicals, they are field and livestock boundaries, they even increase nearby crop yields through their mycorrhizal activity (the hedge effect). But hedges are also a massively underestimated habitat in their own right. They are a perfect blend of woodland, scrub and meadow habitats, supporting species that may be struggling to find these habitats locally. Also bats use hedges to navigate, so if you want more bats, you need lots of bugs and healthy hedges.

Good hedgerows should have a variety of shrub and tree species for a variety of fruiting and flowering times (study them in spring or autumn where the different species are easy to tell apart). They should be cut on a two plus year rotation to maximise flowers and fruit. Aim for a blunt-topped A shape, and cut 10 cm further out from the last cut. When the hedge starts to grow up enough to get 'leggy' at the bottom, it will need relaying, coppicing or require some supportive infill planting.

Hedges are so useful that they are one of the few habitats, (possibly standing water like ponds too), where there is a good argument for regular management even if you have a very hands-off rewilding ethos. This is especially true around non-natural land use on site like farming or hospitality. However, where you have a wild site with habitats forming a varied mosaic, you may get away with letting your hedges overgrow because the wilder site will provide more cover generally for animals. Just remember, unmanaged they will eventually become treelines losing some of their functionality. Plus you will need to manage them more on roadsides, as stock barriers and around public rights of way (PRoW).

To make your hedges gold standard, consider allowing them to bow out in places to form headlands that stick out into the field. Think about the habitat mix in a headland - is it just a meadow headland into a lawn or arable/pasture field, or will it have scrub too? Maybe it could have a pond or scrape at its heart, maybe a large tree. Headlands make excellent stepping stones along the hedge corridor, and in their own right across the landscape. You can do them along streams (riparian corridors) too.

As well as the core shrub species that form a hedge, don't neglect the woodland or meadow features. Good hedges should have hedgerow trees, not just big standards, but a range of future generations, preferably every 10m or so. How many hedges have you seen with admirable big trees, but no saplings or smaller trees coming up past hedge height to future proof the hedge?

As we said previously, hedges are one of the places that trees can grow to vast size with minimal competition, forming amazing habitat features, with even more niches for overnight roosts, food and shelter than the hedge they overshadow. Bear in mind internal hedges will likely provide less future risk to the public with respect to thrown limbs etc. than roadside hedges.

Hedges often have a fascinating field layer of flowering plants under its edge and if allowed, form a margin along the hedge featuring woodland edge species such as foxgloves and hedge parsley. This layer often gains significant height during summer and so supplements the cover aspect of hedgerows as corridors to smaller animals. Additionally, this mixture of both habitat and plant communities in close proximity, mean species like butterflies that may have different food plants at different stages of their lifecycle are often catered for. Don't forget you can supplement these margins with seed planting where necessary - you may need to provide some bare earth scrapes to seeds into. These hedge margins can be useful sources of invertebrates for both pollination and pest control of crops, whilst providing a great buffet for birds, bats and small mammals like shrews.

Meadowlands

Meadows are vital ecosystems that serve as a sanctuary for an array of plant and animal species. They are typically composed of grasses and flowering plants, providing habitats and resources for pollinators like bees and butterflies, birds, and small mammals. Meadows also play a critical role in water management, soil stabilisation, and carbon sequestration.

However, many meadows around the world have been lost due to urban development and intensive agriculture. In the UK we have lost 97% of our traditional meadows.

Naturally maximising the plant diversity is key to success, however a meadow is not a very 3D structural habitat, so optimal results come from creating habitat mosaics, maybe by introducing standard trees to produce wood pasture, and/or adding scrub.

Meadows provide essential ecosystem services such as carbon sequestration, water filtration and storage, aiding flood control. Most of these services are a result of the interplay between plants and their grassland soils, which we'll discuss in more detail later.

Meadows offer aesthetic and recreational opportunities, and contribute to the overall well-being of people who live near them.

Existing Seed Banks

One of the key elements of rewilding meadows is harnessing existing seed banks. Whilst reseeding or supplementary seeding is often necessary, and the biodiversity crisis steers us towards quick impacts, we need to walk a line that allows space for existing plants and seeds. These seed banks are reservoirs of native plant seeds found in the soil or in nearby areas, that theoretically can be direct lineages back to our mesolithic steppes. (Or at least contained 70% of that reservoir into the 1940's before intensive agriculture and herbicides held sway). Seed banks can play a crucial role in restoring the biodiversity and natural processes of meadows. You can very easily give such pioneers the opportunity to come back by removing nutrients (allow weeds to grow for a season or three, cutting and removing late summer until they are less vigorous and the nutrients are gone), then providing some unseeded bare earth scrapes where regeneration can happen. Then see what germinates for a few years. Existing meadows in proximity can also serve as sources of seeds. By utilising both existing seed banks and reseeding, restoration projects can encourage the return of native plants and promote a diverse, self-sustaining meadow ecosystem.

Sowing Seeds

As we discussed above, sowing seeds is a central part of rewilding meadows when natural regeneration alone may not be enough. This process involves introducing native seeds to enhance biodiversity and restore ecological functions, like teasels, and other winter seed plants as a food source for overwintering birds. It's important to select seeds from native plants that are adapted to local conditions as we have already discussed. This can include a mix of grasses, flowering plants, and other species suited to the specific meadow environment. The mixes are normally either 100% wildflower mixes, which are more ornamental, often including annuals that won't return, but are great for public engagement or high impact/aesthetic areas or 80:20% or 70:30% mixes of grasses to wildflowers, which are far more realistic meadow proportions, and far more natural for grazing and biodiversity.

Seeds are typically sown in late summer or early autumn, well before the first frost, when soil conditions are favourable and there is sufficient moisture. They can be spread by hand, using seed spreaders, or by mechanical equipment for larger areas. It's essential to ensure even distribution and sufficient ground preparation to promote healthy plant growth. After sowing, the meadow may require some initial maintenance, such as watering or controlling invasive species, to support the establishment of the new plants.

In following years, you can cut some or all of the meadow from late July to late August to ensure your flowers return the following year. Make sure you remove the cuttings (maybe make a habitat pile in a place you don't mind some nettles next year) or you'll get taller dominant stuff next year.

If you are going for a nature-led, rewilding approach, you can release the herbivores to eat off some of the growth so a patchwork of flowers and taller ruderal stuff comes back next year. You could even just leave it completely, then find your inner pig and turn some of the ground in winter or spring, to provide for next season's low growing wildflowers.

Some further important points for trees, hedges and meadows

Try to plant a variety of species to create diversity. Each planted species will have its own community of plants and animals associated with it, so the more variety you plant, the more species you attract.

This is golden rule number one in nature: the greater diversity that you create - of structure, of habitat, of niches, of species - the greater variety of species and abundance of animals and plants you will attract. So for the most rich and effective natural site - mix it up.

Returning to variation, if you plant more species of plants, you will support mammal, bird and invertebrate species that need a range of fruiting and flowering times to make it through the season.

Try to keep your species mix realistic for the surrounding area, so that you support the plant and animal communities in the landscape that your site sits in. For example is it appropriate to plant a beech wood when there's birch, pine and heather heath all around? No, birch woods, maybe with some pine, and the odd beech would be more supportive to the surrounding wildlife.

Whether you are looking at trees, hedges or meadows there is one common rule I would strongly recommend you heed. Always try to source seeds, plug plants or saplings that *originate* from as close to your site as possible. It's called provenance, and it means that local plants will have closely evolved with the local climate, landscape and wildlife. For example if you plant British bluebells, they will have quirks that benefit local bumblebees, that a Dutch strain of the same bluebell species may not.

So there's a ladder of provenance to remember, going from best to worst:

- On site is the gold standard
- Local area next
- Then from the same landscape (e.g. Somerset Levels)
- Then from the same part of the country e.g. Northumberland
- Then national for the site's soil/sun/shade needs (British hedgerow wildflower mix)
- Then if you can't duck it, or you are experimenting, international sources, (but be careful to not use invasive alien species that get into the wider environment, like rhododendron)

There are nurseries (including online) that specialise in providing local provenance seeds and saplings. But for the really local stuff, search for trees or hedge plants in your vicinity from which you can gather seeds, (digging up wildflowers is often illegal, whereas seed gathering isn't). Talk to any local hay meadows where you can take seeds or better still green cuttings (usually best at the end of July or early August so that most plants have set seed).

Soils

Okay, so maybe it's a six and a half step guide, because soil is a vital component of natural habitats, which I had to shoehorn in somewhere. Hence soil health is a critical aspect of rewilding to provide a foundation for plant growth and sustain the entire meadow ecosystem. Moreover, whether it's for meat, carbs, dairy or vegetables, the vast majority of our food is entirely dependent on soil to grow.

Enhancing soil health can be achieved through practices such as allowing plant growth and herbivory, and reducing soil disturbance.

Having greater plant growth on land means their roots penetrate the soil to various species-dependant depths, so they both help bind the soil together, preventing erosion, nutrient loss and pollution runoff, and they also introduce gaps in the soil, allowing far greater water infiltration, and thus water holding capacity on the land, reducing flood risk and again preventing runoff.

The problem with more plant cover is the creation of more nutrients in the soil when those plants die, which wildflowers don't favour, but nettles, thistles and docks do. The answer is herbivores. Grazers remove the nutrients and so restore some balance back to wildflowers and hence pollinators. Yes they dung out some nutrients, but obviously less than they take in, or they wouldn't grow.

Disturbance wrecks soil structure reducing the water holding and nutrient provision of soils. So stopping or limiting ploughing, where avoidable is admirable. However, we mustn't forget that some level of soil disturbance is natural in an ecosystem that evolved alongside wild boar, so low density pigs as proxies, or mimicry with some random turning over of the top 9-12" (23-30cm) of soil in patches is ideal, and strikes a balance between undisturbed soils, and creating bare earth scrapes for wildflower germination, so they can compete with dominant species.

Step Two - animals

Herbivores

Let's just for a moment, linger on plants again. Now what I didn't mention in section one, is that plants want to grow. The taller they grow the more sun they get, and that powers everything they do, so it's important. However, just when they are basking in the light, another species comes along and shades them out. Then the same thing happens to that plant. And so on until canopy trees shade everything out. This is called plant succession.

Now this may sound obvious but herbivores eat plants. And the more plants they eat, the less plants there are. (I told you it was basic). So if we have lots of herbivores, we end up with just short plants and grasses and plant succession never takes off; as anything not adapted to being eaten doesn't get the chance to grow. So if you look at most shaved sheep pastures, you get the idea.

However, if you are the only cow in the field, you can't eat everything. There may be the odd patch you keep trimmed, but on the whole, nettles, brambles, hawthorn and oaks (exact species depending on your soils and location) will progress and take over. Fast forward 30 years and you'll have a young woodland.

Therefore, as we said before, the greatest results for nature come when we have a diversity of habitat. Therefore better than woodland or grassland is a mixture of the two. Something called wood pasture (that looks like an unmowed version of country house parkland - big trees, little copses, patches of scrub, surrounded by lightly grazed meadow). Actually if you think about it, grazed orchards fulfil much the same purpose; as does grazed agroforestry.

Naturally it is excellent to create some core woodland and meadow habitat, if you have space. However for the majority that don't, wood pasture is an excellent mixed option, in the same way that hedges are a mixture of different habitats. In fact even if you do have loads of space, there is plenty of evidence that wood pasture would have formed a significant portion of our ancient landscapes, so I would recommend using it to transition between woodland and grassland areas anyway. It is a way to make your site even richer.

Anyway, back to those herbivores, because we need them to create these mosaic landscapes. On a practical front it's important to get the stocking level right for the area, for the habitat type, and the soil type. As a rule of thumb, the wetter the ground, the more plant eating animals it will support, as plants will grow quicker. And you are better to start low and build your stock holding up, than to go in with loads of animals, decimate the place and have to remove animals.

Naturally, if you are trying to make a living from the stock, you may have to compromise between optimal habitat management stocking levels and keeping enough stock to farm - so your habitats will by default be more grassland. Here it is important to concentrate on hedges, trees, zoning areas off from grazing and playing with grazing rotations to rest grasslands. It might be worth looking at native breeds that are far less delicate with respect to the forage they munch. These breeds may overwinter outdoors and more rarely require supplementary feeding. This will lower your bills to go some way to compensating for lower stocking levels, and will reduce the requirement for such a high percentage of land use to produce supplementary feed, in the UK and beyond. And consider the potential of pasture fed or premium quality meat markets.

So what animals do we mean by herbivores? Well there are some wild herbivores out there. The most common ones are mice, voles, deer, rabbits, hares and geese. It's rare that any of these over graze except deer, so we mostly encourage them. However, deer, voles and mice will attack new tree planting, so it's important to guard these. And deer will munch most anything although they are most known for browsing shoots, leaves and stems of trees and bushes, stopping regeneration.

The most popular way to "naturally" control habitats is to use mega herbivores. Now the wild ones are mostly extinct, like aurochs and tarpan. So we use proxies for their role instead, such as domestic cows for their ancient auroch ancestors, and in the same way, horses for tarpan. We are still waiting for wild boar to be recognised as a native species, so in the meantime we use pigs, that dig over the soil in a similar manner, returning the clock of plant succession back to bare earth, to give many types of insects and pioneer wildflowers a chance.

To use herbivores as proxies for lost species, it's important to understand their feeding habits and hence their effect on habitat.

Cattle tear bunches of grass with their prehensile tongue. They feed in a piecemeal fashion across a grassland and leave a longer sward (height of grades and meadow flowers), than other species. This naturally leaves a diverse grassland behind them, more prone to succeeding to scrub in parts, if the stocking level is low.

Sheep nibble delicately close to the ground so leave quite a lawn behind them. However, they are pickier than most, so if some taller or woodier plants and grass tussocks have already established, the sheep may leave them until last. So again stocking levels and rotations are key to your outcomes. It's useful to bear in mind that one cow is roughly equivalent to 12 sheep in effect.

Horses eat like sheep, but they are equivalent in appetite to a cow, so they actually eat like 12 sheep. They have the unusual habit of dunging and urinating in the same patches. You often get big nettle and dock patches where these nutrients are. However, this is excellent for the rest of the site, where nutrients are kept low. Unlike sheep and cattle that distribute more widely.

Goats are escape artists that famously eat anything, so fencing is a key consideration. However, being small they are a practical choice for some gardens, but watch them around new planting. Plus they are not waterproof, so they need shelter.

Domestic geese and rabbits could also be used in gardens, although they can be a bit picky, and definitely require a degree of looking after.

This last point is key to taking on any stock, even in a garden. What are you going to do with the geese when you go on holiday? What will you do with your cattle? You and others may need training. You need most stock registered with various DEFRA departments and the vet. You *may* need drinking troughs and filler pipes, supplementary feed stations, vehicles, barns, hard standing areas, gates and fencing. It's not for the faint hearted, it's a thorough responsibility, not least from an animal welfare perspective. Therefore it really isn't for everyone, and must never be undertaken lightly or without lots of advice, both from experts, but also from other people that are doing it.

However, please weigh this up with the knowledge that using real herbivores is by far the most natural way to allow nature to rebound, and will have the most realistic outcome.

So what can you do if you can't use herbivore proxies? Well don't worry you still have options. And the main one is mimicry. Here *you* take on the role of the missing animals. How? Well here are a few ideas:

- Sheep/cow = strimmer or sickle - try different heights (short sward for a sheep and longer for a cow) and a random distribution, some scattered, some concentrated in one area.
- Sheep/horse = mower - to create more intensely grazed lawns
- Wild boar/pig = shovel - turn over the surface to a depth of between 9-12" exposing the naked earth beneath. Again random is the name of the game. Boar rootle around haphazardly here and there searching for food, but then when they find something it's like the Somme or Glastonbury - mud everywhere. Plus they will only turn moist soil in woods, and fields during the wetter months. So you don't need to go breaking your back.

- Deer = secateurs - they browse the tender ends of stems, shoots and leaves; they are nature's pruners
- Beavers = chainsaw/loppers/axe - they chop trees down near water allowing more light into the habitat. They often move those trees into the streams to help form leaky dams and upstream ponds. The stumps often coppice, i.e. throw up a multitude of stems creating a new scrubby habitat. They also strip bark creating beaver chips that mulch down enriching the soils. Additionally beavers strip smaller branches and twigs to fill gaps in their dams. Sometimes they excavate side channels that bypass the dam to relieve pressure on the dam during times of flood. You can do all of this if you like.
- Elephant/rhino = chainsaw - no I've not lost the plot, we actually had these creatures before the last ice age, and woolly versions during the ice ages. Why do you think most of our native trees grow back loads of new stems if you chop them down (coppice)? Not to deal with a land full of badgers and cattle, that's for sure. So elephants and rhinos rub against trees and remove the bark (axe). Boar do too, but obviously lower down. Elephants and rhino fell trees to reach the leaves, which naturally lets light into the woodland understory. Sometimes they break the trunk, but a bit of the original remains intact, so the fallen tree still grows.

There is one site in the UK that has reintroduced our once native European bison into a woodland habitat in Kent, breaking down small trees and distributing seeds in their dung. And who knows, maybe one day we'll see elk and reindeer back. So the last thing we'll discuss are reintroductions.

So this is where you reintroduce an extinct or missing species. It needs to be a native species, not an aardvark or gibbon. And it is a guaranteed headline grabber. However, this is another approach that isn't always for the faint hearted; with some species it will take time and money. But where there's a will there's a way.

You need to do feasibility studies, liaise with all manner of stakeholders, from national bodies like the Environment Agency, DEFRA and Natural England, to the local community and neighbouring land owners, maybe the press too. And sometimes you may have a battle on your hands. Beavers have quite notably roused anger and stubborness amongst farmers and anglers, even though the science is all in favour of beavers benefiting fish, and there's some pretty simple mitigation techniques for protecting agricultural drainage and trees from them.

But the result of returning an original species can be vast, because not only do they fulfil the roles you expect, but often unlooked for ones like seed dispersal and disturbance. You are filling in all those lost links in ecological networks, where different species interact with each other.

Successful UK herbivore reintroductions include: bison, water voles, great bustard, beavers, bitterns and chequered skipper butterflies.

Whilst I respect that species reintroduction is a step beyond what most people would feel to be feasible, there's no reason not to help provide habitat for species reintroduced into your vicinity. For example, if you want water fowl in winter, and you are lucky enough to have the space and money to create a lake, then build islands or rafts to give the birds a sense of security from foxes, stoats and weasels, that might predate them, or their eggs.

Predators

If you eat prey, that makes you a carnivore (eats animals), or an omnivore (eats plants and animals). So all the nutrients and energy that herbivores get from plants, are in turn gained by predators when they eat herbivores, or when they eat other predators too.

Now as far as working with predators goes, we are more limited than with herbivores to be honest. But don't worry, there are some options. There are definitely some naturally occurring ones that we can provide for, to increase their impact. And if nothing else we can always try to do some mimicry.

Reintroduction of predators has been limited to creatures with very specialist habitat or location requirements, such as natterjack toads, pool frogs, sand lizards and smooth snakes. Pine marten, osprey, white tailed sea eagles and wild cats are equally challenging due to stakeholder objections, so unless you live in areas where these are already reintroduced and recovering you can do little to support this. Red kites and otters have been very successful however, spreading over large areas, so you may be able to support those with favourable habitat and feeding opportunities.

And providing support is the key to helping existing predators, and diversifying your plot. First find out what is present in your neighbourhood. You may see foxes, badgers, hedgehogs or birds of prey (raptors). So find out what their food, water and shelter requirements are and do your best to provide those on site.

Another option is to ask either the local Wildlife Trust, or an ecologist, or check out (and learn to use) NBN Atlas website in the UK, which the first two will probably refer to anyway. NBN Atlas tells you all the different species spotted in your vicinity, ever. The last point is key, you may want to filter your search to the last five years so you don't get animals spotted in the 80's.

Then do a bit of ecology research online, and you'll soon find out how to encourage hedgehogs to your patch for example. Most predators will require a varied diet of other species to thrive, so you can cover the food angle, by working on creating varied habitats to attract many species. From a shelter point of view, again the more varied habitat the better, because you are likely to cover the housing requirements of many species. And water is pretty universal, although a choice of watering holes is desirable if you have space, to save predators and prey drinking cheek by jowl. So as you can see, working on your mosaic habitats and water features is universal for helping animal diversity.

However, some species have more exacting needs, but you can still do something about that.

Let's take raptors as an example. Most feed on small mammals, amphibians, other birds and carrion. So with tall field margins or meadows, hedges and scrub, you are really fulfilling their food needs. But taking it a step further; what sets raptors apart as a predator? They rely on their phenomenal sense of sight to spot prey. So if you construct platforms - raptor posts - from which they can survey the meadow etc. you are likely to attract them. You are not only providing dinner, but you are also making it very easy for them to succeed.

Another example for those in the southeast of England, you may want to consider building stork nest platforms to attract our returning white storks. They mooch through meadows, wet meadows and shallow ponds and marshes for prey (amphibians, small mammals and the eggs of ground nesting birds), so providing these habitats would be highly attractive to a white stork.

If the opportunity comes up to petition for, or get involved in removing a weir downstream of your stretch of water, you will benefit fish, helping them reach your waterways, and thereby attract otters. (And kingfishers, herons, and maybe even overwintering cormorants).

Mimicry of predators is limited but there are some options. Firstly, think about what the role of a predator in the landscape is; what do we want to achieve? Well I guess the prime job of predators as we have already alluded, is to eat herbivores. Well from an ecological point of view, if herbivore numbers drop, job done. So if you have domestic livestock, and some are sold when finished, then you are both turning a profit (hopefully), and acting as a predator. If you don't want to sell the animals, then maybe rotating where they feed (or better still, where some of them feed) will have a similar effect.

Now to mimic this effect on wild animals is naturally much tougher. In fact, rabbits, hares, voles, red squirrels and mice are hardly thriving so the last thing I want to do is encourage anybody to harm them. However, there is a very strong case for deer control in the UK. In fact it is already happening to the tune of 350,000 animals culled per year, but their population is still increasing, in the absence of natural predators. There is a strong consensus that they could form a very sustainable source of wild harvest, like sea fish. And in fact they are already being sold in such a manner by many specialist UK outlets.

Another role of predators is to vary the feeding distribution of herbivores by influencing where, when and how they feed, through their presence generating fear amongst their prey. This is called the landscape of fear. And it is relatively easy to create. To start with, what predator are you mimicking: a wolf, a lynx or an eagle? Eagles and wolves feed in the open, so you would want your herbivores (and their effects) concentrated close to cover. However, lynx are woodland ambush predators, so roe deer (their choice prey) would probably avoid staying near the edges.

Next, how does your herbivore act? Some like rabbits always stay close to cover in case they have to bolt, so rabbit lawns tend to occur closer to cover. Deer, cattle and horses tend to depend on herd dynamics. Smaller deer tend to have smaller herds and so stay close to cover, even roe, since they have lived without lynx for too long. Larger deer like fallow and red tend to form larger family herds with lots of eyes so feel safe in the open, as do lone mature stags, although remember as browsers most of their food is among scrub, hedges and woods. Things tend to work likewise for families of cattle and horses. And wild boar do have a tendency to avoid more open spaces like cropland in wolf dominated areas.

So now you need to work out how to transfer these effects onto your herbivores. You could fence off areas that are less likely to be grazed when imaginary predators are present. Or you could use visual (like model animals, kites, scarecrows) or auditory deterrents (like predator recordings or loud bangs) to encourage animals to avoid certain areas.

Scavengers and decomposers

Many people forget what an essential function these creatures and fungi perform. What do you think gets rid of all the dead bodies and dung in the environment? What recycles all the nutrients from that dung and those carcasses, making them once more available for plants to grow with?

What would it look like without them? Well we'd have a landscape full of dead bodies and poo. Nice. As it is, many of these species are repressed through our biosecurity - not leaving carcasses of domestic animals in the environment to feed this vital guild of creatures. Then our pet and livestock worming products poison the dung beetles so few survive to break down our dog poo and cow pats, meaning it lasts far longer before bacteria and fungi can finish the job.

So here we are talking about foxes, the crow family, some raptors, and then invertebrates like dung beetles, flies, other beetles and butterflies.

So how can we cater for this macabre but fascinating necrobiome on our site?
Well primarily by not killing them through pesticide and wormer use (discussed further in step 5). But the other principle action you can take is actually to provide scavenging opportunities on your plot.

I'm not suggesting you buy prime rib eye for wildlife. However, you could ask for offcuts from the butcher, or even gather up some fresher roadkill, but please don't get knocked down yourself, and you may get some interesting questions from the butcher or passersby.

Then distribute these offerings about your site periodically. If you have a small garden, I can understand you not wanting the smell especially near the house or frequented parts of the garden. But once you start catering to the clean up crew, they will come. So in theory, the more you encourage them, the less time the carrion will take to decompose.

One forward thinking rewilder builds giant tables, eight feet off the ground to discourage terrestrial scavengers, and leaves this buffet to help raptors like buzzards, red kites, goshawks and others. Personally I feel there should be a sharing option on the ground too, so no one is left out of this smorgasbord.

Invertebrates

Now invertebrates are literally anything without a backbone, from molluscs like squid and slugs, crustaceans like crabs or woodlice, arachnids like spiders or the myriad of different types of worms. However, by far the most abundant class of invertebrate on earth, with an estimated 5.5 million different species, are the arthropods, or insects.

Described by one of the greatest biologists of all time, EO Wilson, as the little things that run the world, we certainly are lost without them. They pollinate plants providing you with one in every three mouthfuls of food. Also, as described above they are fundamental for returning the nutrients from dung and dead plants and animals to the ground, without which new plants have nothing to grow with. Furthermore they are great pest controllers, keeping plague proportions of some of their own populations in check, protecting our crops from pests like locusts or colorado beetles.

To help insects, you need to think at a microhabitat level. That means that you need to see your site from a beetle or bee's eye view. Insects are no different to any other animals, they need food, water and shelter. The difficulty with insects is that they don't all fly, and not all that do, fly far. So the more habitat and resource options there are on a small scale, the greater range of insects you will support.

Now strictly speaking there are herbivorous insects that belong in the last chapter, but the majority are omnivores, carnivores, or even have different feeding habits in different stages of their life cycle. Additionally, many are parasitic to each other. The vast majority of what insects consume, apart from plant material, are other insects. Therefore, by actioning ways to help insects, increases insect numbers, which in turn helps all but herbivorous insects. So it is a positive, largely self-sustaining, cycle.

So therefore, diet takes care of itself, and hence if you get the habitats right the rest will follow. And as insects are so diverse, they live in all habitats, so whatever you do in the way of habitats should be positive. However, as always the more variety the better, plus there are certain habitats that are gold standard with respect to insects. These are:

- Meadows with a variable height sward, that isn't all cut back at the end of summer, with plenty of flowers for pollinators;
- Standing or fallen deadwood is essential to nearly 1500 species of UK insects and should be left in place if possible - however in a garden, where you don't need a dead branch clonking anyone on the head, maybe make bug houses or stacked log piles;

- Bare earth is vital to many species of beetle and solitary mining bees - south facing, bare earth or sandy banks are best as they make warm homes , and also make excellent pest control features, especially in arable fields.
- Also don't forget water; not only is it necessary for aquatic species like dragonflies, queens and kings of the aerial hunt, but also for all the other invertebrates.
    - You may want to add some gravel and stones to a gentle slope on one part of your pond, so that invertebrates can get water without falling in
    - Now you may have a beautiful pond, but is it any use to a beetle on the other side of the field? Consider seasonal scrapes that hold water, tyre tracks from farm machinery may suffice and hoofprints of your herbivores too. Maybe you can poach the ground in the same manner yourself if you have no livestock, with a pick or a mattock. Even cow pats can provide insects with water.

Other roles

Now the one paramount, and most often forgotten about natural process, is disturbance. In fact, in a 2018 scientific study into the essential components of nature recovery, disturbance was one of only three fundamental factors found to be necessary, along with diversity and distribution (connectivity).

So why are we discussing this in the animal section of the book? Well the majority of disturbance to normalise on site is of animal origin. Don't get me wrong you can chop a tree down every ten years in the woods like a hurricane, to let in more light, or seasonally top up your pond to overflowing like a flood, but let's face it, that is going to happen anyway these days, at least twice a year! You don't really need to mimic natural events that are already happening. But there are plenty of animals that create disturbance, which unless you have them already, you can mimic.

The main ones are badgers, boar, beavers, bison and elephants. Yes, elephants. Our landscapes really miss the actions of the huge herbivores - rhino and elephant - so anything we can do to bring back/mimic their *role*, without having the actual animals terrorise motorists on the M4, is fantastic.

Badgers, and foxes too, create tunnels and bolt holes, which can be quite erosive to sandy soils, and create that excellent sandbank habitat discussed above in the invertebrate section. Tunnels may be hard to replicate, but digging complexes of deep holes are certainly possible. And who knows, where you dig, the real diggers may follow.

Boar we have discussed elsewhere. They turn over moist grassland and woodland floors searching for grubs, worms, roots and tubers. So turn over both piecemeal, and more continuous areas of soil. They also create muddy wallows, especially in woodland, which they love, but which also provide vital water for other species especially during droughts. That shouldn't be too tough to replicate on larger sites with woods. More challenging perhaps is the ability of the boar's bristly coat and digestive tract in transferring seeds across miles, to help the spread of plants. You could drag an old carpet about I guess, but if you could replicate the stimulating effect of a boar's bowel on seeds, quite apart from the transport function, it would probably make you a leader in this field.

Elephants we covered in the herbivore section. So it's scraping off bark and chopping down trees, SPARINGLY, and with the aim to let them coppice from the stump. So first research which of your trees coppice, as these would be most appropriate to fell, having evolved around these mega-megaherbivores. You can randomly pick your chainsaw victim, or be a bit cheeky and work out where the extra light works best, before chopping. And I say sparingly because if you have a 500 acre wood, then you can afford to be a bit gung ho, whereas if you have less than 50 trees, you may begrudge losing one. You can always experiment with a partial cut that stays slightly attached to the stump when cut. If you (or an expert) succeed, you may have a tree that grows from several points along the trunk. Please contact the local council if you are unsure whether any tree preservation orders (TPOs) are in place BEFORE you damage anything, and please don't fell any present or future veteran trees.

Bison fell small trees and scrub (mainly through rubbing against them), spread seeds in their dung, and like stallions and bulls, create dust wallows (bull pits). These are shallow depressions of bare earth, again fantastic for bugs, and again fairly easy to recreate. The broken scrub and small trees can be achieved with loppers, axes and saws. Breaks probably occur at varying heights depending on the size of the slouching bison. Don't forget with felled trees to leave the dead wood where it falls if possible, only tidying into a log pile if health and safety necessitates.

Finally, there's beavers. And again we discussed them in herbivores. So you can fell trees near wetlands to coppice the stumps and let in light to the area. Then the dead wood can be trimmed or manipulated across streams to create leaky dams.

Twigs and branches from trees can be used to make the dam more effective. Chippings of wood and bark, can be left to mulch around the stump as beavers would, to provide nutrients for other plants. (I know, the opposite of wildflower advice, but hey it's what happens). And beavers sometimes excavate side channels that allow *some* water to overflow and protect their dams from being damaged by really strong floods. So if you like, feel free to get your shovels out. But don't forget the overall aim is to hold up the water so it releases water gradually during times of heavy or prolonged rainfall. Therefore, these side channels should be small, and beavers only make them if they have to, so check how the dam functions before going down that road.

Step Three - water

Every living thing needs water to survive. Terrestrial wildlife, aerial wildlife, livestock and especially aquatic wildlife all rely on proximity to water. So by restoring or introducing water features onto your site, you are very simply going to improve nature on site. Plus without nature there to filter our water, to drive the water cycle, we wouldn't be here either.

Drainage

For centuries, drainage systems have been installed in fields to facilitate agricultural activities. By channelling excess water away from fields, these systems make the land more suitable for farming by reducing waterlogging and increasing crop yields. However, as modern agriculture expanded, these practices often led to significant ecological changes, including habitat destruction, soil degradation, and loss of biodiversity.

Removing drainage allows fields to revert to their natural state, promoting the return of wetlands, marshes, and other aquatic habitats, particularly at the bottom of any slopes, providing critical homes for a wide variety of native plant and animal species, many of which are rare or endangered, all of which contribute to a richer, more balanced environment.

Wetlands are also known to capture and store carbon, helping to mitigate climate change, and by reconnecting these fields to their floodplains, you restore natural water cycles, improving water quality by filtering out pollutants and sediments, benefiting both the environment and communities downstream. Additionally, rewetting fields can create landscapes that are more resilient to changing weather patterns, such as floods and droughts, by providing natural water retention areas.

The process of drainage removal and rewetting fields can be costly, including the physical work of removing infrastructure and restoring the landscape and may conflict with existing agricultural activities. Farmers may consider adapting their practices or transitioning to more water tolerant crops.

Find details on how and where to destroy or block field drains by using that search on the gov.uk website.

Existing rivers and lakes

To restore nature along or around any existing water features, is of paramount importance, because you really want to maximise the impact of those aquatic, marginal and riparian habitats. To do this, there are a variety of appropriate approaches you can take depending on the health of these habitats. Here are some specific actions that can be taken:

- Rewilding the riparian zones (the areas along the banks of rivers and ponds) by planting native vegetation can help stabilise banks, filter runoff, and provide habitat for wildlife. This also helps shade the water and maintain cooler temperatures which can be vital to some spawning fish species. If livestock are poaching (eroding) the shores, you may need to fence off the water bodies until the vegetation is established (naturally these animals will need other water sources). Bear in mind that as well as the banks, for which you can think of water loving tree species, like alder and willow maybe, and maybe water tolerant seed mixes, you can also plant marginal and aquatic species too. You can get marginal seed and plug plant mixes from native plant nurseries.
- Identifying and removing invasive plant and animal species from rivers and ponds, as in

any habitat, is crucial for allowing native species to thrive. If you are planting in and around streams, be particularly careful with biosecurity - any introduced non-native species, such as floating pennywort or Australian stonecrop, could easily move down river, and nigh on impossible to remove, for which you would be responsible. Mention your concerns to your plant nursery before buying.
- Rewilding efforts often involve the reintroduction of native species that have been extirpated from the area. Don't forget that this can include the small things, such as fish, amphibians, plants and other aquatic organisms, as well as that poster child, the beaver. We cover more about reintroductions in Chapter 2: Animals, but for thorough advice contact Rewilding Britain.
- Dams and weirs can disrupt the natural flow of rivers and prevent fish and invertebrates, like crayfish, from migrating. Modifying or removing these structures can restore the natural flow and improve habitat connectivity. However, their destruction can also affect local water abstraction and even lead to greater risk of flooding downstream, so please seek expert hydrology advice and liaise with all the statutory bodies, and possibly other stakeholders, beforehand.
- Enhancing the structural complexity of rivers, by rewriggling them, (with one or several

diggers), creating pools, side channels, oxbows and backwaters off the main channels, can really increase the dynamism of artificially straightened rivers. River meanders start to form their own undercut banks on the outside of bends, and beaches on the inside, all really valuable habitat. Don't just think about the 2D complexity of the river but think about the riverbed profile too. Creating deeper pools, shallow riffles, gravel beds, and promoting natural sedimentation patterns (which will naturally follow any rewiggling efforts), can create diverse habitats for different species. Think carefully about removing any bank reinforcement to improve this, but weigh it up with the potential for further erosion, and as always explore the up and downstream repercussions of any actions before starting work, taking advice as necessary.

- Adding fallen timber to streams and rivers can divert flows or create leaky dams that allow valuable wetland pools to form up behind them - an especially useful action in the absence of beavers.
- Many of these actions, in turn, allow rivers to overflow onto their natural floodplains, creating dynamic wetland habitats for a variety of species and improve flood resilience downstream. So tie the actions of the previous points, to creating extra pools, ditches, channels and planting schemes in

fields alongside rewiggled streams and rivers, or behind leaky dams to create complex wetlands in times of flood, to tie up the water, and also to hold onto the water when the flood recedes, so that the aquatic habitat persists. What earth is dug out can be used to make mounds that make good island habitats when it floods. See them as stepping stones through the seasonal marshes. You could possibly plant them up with willows and marginals.

- Finally, depending on pond size and your site ethos, plan occasional future clearance every few years, as ponds tend to silt up over time. Purist rewilders may want the shrinking ponds as a feature in their own right - and rightly natural. However, balance this against the quantity and value of water on site - it would be a shame to lose that at some point in the future. It's always best to leave all the smelly arisings from the pond bed alongside the pond for a few days to give any aquatic species removed a chance to return to the pond.

All these actions work best when combined and tailored to the specific characteristics of the river or pond in question, and in the case of rivers and streams, when implemented in partnership with local stakeholders such as landowners, conservation organisations, and government agencies, where applicable.

New scrapes and ponds

Creating new scrapes and ponds is a key part of rewilding efforts, as they provide critical habitats for wildlife and help restore natural water systems. They are incredibly important in areas with no existing water features on site, but can also be useful to supplement present water bodies.

Scrapes and ponds create a variety of habitats (aquatic, marginal, marsh, bog, fen, carr woodland) that support different species, including amphibians, birds, insects, and plants. These water features offer food, shelter, and breeding grounds for many species, promoting overall biodiversity. Scrapes and ponds can also help manage water runoff and improve groundwater recharge. They act as reservoirs, slowing down the flow of water across the landscape, reducing erosion and preventing flooding in lower-lying areas. Not only that, but they can help improve water quality by acting as natural filters. Vegetation around the water bodies can trap sediments and pollutants, leading to cleaner water downstream. And don't forget that ponds enhance the visual appeal of the landscape and provide opportunities for recreational activities such as birdwatching, photography, and walks. It's a well known fact that time in nature improves your mental health, but not as many people realise that time by water also helps us. So creating wetland features is doubly supportive for people on the site.

- First, choose a location that can support a water body, considering factors such as soil type, topography, and proximity to existing water sources. Sandy soils may only support ponds when lined with clay (or artificial liners if all else fails). Avoid areas with existing high-value habitats that could be negatively impacted by the new feature.
- The size and depth of the scrape or pond will depend on the goals of the rewilding project and the species you wish to attract. Smaller, shallower scrapes are ideal for amphibians and wading birds, while deeper ponds can support fish and larger aquatic species. In an ideal world you can have a pond with a variety of types of depth profile.
- Think about slopes vs. banks too - can terrestrial species escape up a slope (ducks and many waders like to waddle up a slope too). Plus this encourages a range of plant and animal species to inhabit the area.
- Scrapes will dry up in hot weather, whereas deeper ponds shouldn't. Don't let this overly trouble you, many species live or rely on what we call the drop-down zone, that floods, then dries out seasonally. (However, if you only have scrapes, you may have nothing aquatic left to give animals sanctuary during a drought).

- Plant native vegetation around the edges of the water body to stabilise the soil and provide habitat for wildlife. Again choose marginal plants or those that can tolerate wet conditions and that are suitable for the soil, sun and region. Keep your eye out for invasive species again too.

Step Four - connections

Scale

This is bound to be a short section, because as far as scale goes, you either have it or you don't. Naturally if you're loaded, expanding your site can be very exciting. Scientifically, greater patch size means you should have more species, greater abundance of individual plants and animals and more scope for variation in habitats. Bigger sites are closer to becoming core habitat sites for wildlife in general after all. However, scaling up is beyond the scope of most people and always difficult to achieve in the UK and northern Europe anyway, due to the population density, infrastructure and urbanisation. There is far greater scope in many southern European countries where rural abandonment is common.

This does highlight how important connectivity is. For places that are too small for reasonable wildlife population sizes, connections to other patches are paramount. And although it's only a rule of thumb, in Blighty, where you have little choice anyway, connectivity can be a proxy for scale. For example two 10 acre sites joined by good nature friendly, functional corridors are effectively one 20 acre site.

Now that's not strictly true. Animals may behave differently in a corridor where predation is more likely than deep in a quiet few acres of woodland.

Nowhere is the issue of connecting plots together more important, or noticeable, than in urban areas. In towns and cities plot sizes are almost always small, so connections between them are of heightened importance. Hedgehog tunnels in fences between properties, permeable fencing, or better still, hedges, take on a whole new level of importance. Forming street or community groups are excellent ways of helping links expand. Connecting into green spaces or arteries, like parks, sports grounds, golf courses, canals and rivers, can really move the urban agenda for nature. As can green roofs, bus shelters, green walls, wild road verges and traffic islands, even planting gaps in pavements.

The aim is to have nature flowing amongst our densest populations so that it becomes part of everyone's everyday, combating the nature disconnect.

Cores, corridors and stepping stones

So what do we mean by cores, corridors or stepping stones?

Well cores are prime areas of at least one, but preferably a mix of habitats. Here nature can be itself, individuals and species mingling, expressing their natural characteristics - feeding, mating, competing, collaborating. Examples could include the Cairngorms Connect scheme within the National Park of the same name. Equally, Wild Ennerdale in the Lake District could be classed as a core for biodiversity, as could Knepp Castle Estate in East Sussex, and numerous large nature reserves across the British Isles. But these beautiful areas of habitat are many miles apart in most cases. So we need to bring them closer together with corridors and stepping stones, and in that way, nature starts to migrate through the landscape.

Corridors are quite self explanatory; complex linear features like hedges, streams (and the channels of vegetation that they sit in), or at sea, reefs, that allow creatures to move from one patch of favourable habitat to another with less risk of predation.

Stepping stones are smaller patches of favourable habitat that species can use as a stop off between core areas. Now you may have seen this coming but this is where you come in. Why? Because, unless you have over 500 acres of land, rewilding, or restoring nature on your land is likely to result in a stepping stone of habitat. But please don't be disheartened, stepping stones are exactly what we need, everywhere. Without them, those core areas are isolated and may as well be zoos, wonderful wild showcases but functionally useless. This is largely how nature reserves have behaved until recent years. We need thousands upon thousands of nature rich, wild patches pinging up all over the place. The more we have, on average, the closer together they become. So then by combining them with corridors, wildlife has the chance to flow between them, or in some cases set up home in them.

And this is a further point, you can use this analogy of cores, corridors and stepping stones at many scales. On the one hand you can use it as above, with large core reserves and estates, then smaller landowners and households providing stepping stones, while ambitious nature corridor schemes, like Weald to Waves in Sussex, that is linking the high Weald near Crawley, across Sussex, to Littlehampton and Newhaven and out into the bay, join everything together. However, on the other hand, you could see two patches of woodland on your land as cores, with a hedgerow corridor between them, and a headland halfway along the hedge as a stepping stone, supporting those species that find traversing the hedge too long for one dash. There again, to other species a diverse headland may be a perfect home, or core habitat, and some will even happily live in the hedge. So to reiterate my point above, do not be disheartened or get imposter syndrome if you are only contributing a third of your garden. Every patch of decent habitat helps. Whilst it may only be a take-away for lunch for some species passing through, it will be a wonderful new home to others.

Another point is to not forget that not all habitats suit all species, so try to study your plot from the perspective of very varied species - birds, bats, flying bugs, walking bugs, large or small, fast or slow mammals. Aquatic species will likely see ponds or streams as core habitat, but can you connect them? Amphibians and most aquatic mammals will move some distance overland in search of water, however fish and most invertebrates can't. The flip side is that you can't win them all; even nature doesn't connect every lake and every pond.

When considering your site's connectivity, I would advise you to think both about on the site, and beyond the site. On site, how do species traverse your site? Do you have streams or hedges, high sward meadows, scrub or woodlands with dense understories? What is the bankside vegetation like? And although we discussed hedges earlier, how functional are they? Do they look dense and bushy, with a good diverse field layer? Do they have a variety of shrubs? Or are they a monoculture, with significant gaps to fill. If you were a woodmouse would you be happy avoiding owls along them? Would you have enough to eat through the season?

Would your site benefit from habitat islands in fields, or headlands along hedges/riparian corridors (waterways)? Site your island midway across the field and it effectively reduces the risk of predation for those prey species seeking to cross.

How helpful is the matrix? Not loads of green data from the film; the matrix is what a creature has to traverse between good habitats. So to reach the next wood they may have to cross a field - what is that field vegetation like? That is the matrix. So a diverse wildflower or hay meadow will be far easier to traverse than a short sward of heavily grazed pasture. Oil seed rape and wheat or barley may be quite tall and provide cover, but may be useless after harvesting. Naturally, a new housing estate will often be even more dangerous to cross, and not a good matrix for species. If you are a developer and can build this level of biological complexity into your site, I applaud you.

If you have a farm, could you chop those bits off fields that create lots of short work, making them unprofitable? Then could you put good habitat in those areas, maybe generating environmental payments? If you have a line of telegraph poles down one field that are a pain to work between, maybe plant a hedge down that line to support wildlife.

Maybe create a south facing, dry earth or sandy bank between the poles to support bees and beetles, then put a hedge on the north side for birds, bats and other creatures. Perhaps a field corner where two hedges meet is a good site for a headland/island of habitat, with minimal disruption to farm work.

After you have brainstormed your site, start to study your site's place in the larger landscape. Where are the nearest nature reserves? Who nearby has done habitat restoration? Where do patches of habitat exist? And what is the nearby habitat like? Different types of habitat have different communities of plants and animals. The occupants of an ancient wood are different to a conifer plantation, are different to wetlands, which are different to chalk grasslands, and are different to orchards or heathland. So think about your site in context. If your plot is completely different to the surrounding habitats, how much help will you be to the species you expect to be nearby. Again however, there are always two sides to consider. Maybe by providing a patch of woodland in the middle of the grasslands of Salisbury Plain, you have created a vital overnight roosting site and feeding station for birds.

You have probably come to realise that there are no absolutes, no right or wrong answers, so usually a bit of common sense goes a long way in nature recovery. Use logic, be pragmatic and you can't go far wrong. So don't panic, it's really hard to get wrong. If things aren't going as you'd expect, talk to an expert. But often just experimenting can help. For example, a good scientific approach is not to put all your eggs in one basket. Don't reseed the entire site. Reseed some bits and dig bare earth scrapes in others to support the existing seed bank. You can always assess what comes up over the next three to four years and work out whether it's worth sticking with both approaches or not. And let's face it, you're not building a concrete car park. Hence, it won't be too difficult to reverse for the first 10-20 years if you change your mind. The worst would be to dig up moderate trees and find where you hid the earth, to fill the pond back in. Don't get me wrong, you'll be off my Christmas list, but it's theoretically pretty easy.

The next thing to consider, after studying your neighbours, is to connect your site to theirs, where possible. So the obvious first steps are physical connections. What are their hedges like, can you help repair them? Same with riparian corridors, maybe even general habitat. If you have a site of special scientific interest (SSSI) half a mile away, that is designated as an SSSI due to its saproxylic (deadwood) beetles, then it would be sensible to look after your veteran and ageing trees, and to leave deadwood in situ to support those often rare beetle communities. The more you connect your site into the landscape surrounding it, the more functional it will become. When you create a local (or larger) network for nature to move around, you really have cracked it. But naturally to succeed at this level you need to talk to people.

Relationships

Probably the most valuable asset anyone has in life, is relationship capital; who you know, and who knows you. And this is particularly true if you want to help nature. Do you think you will have a greater impact if you get on with your neighbours, or if you give each other a wide berth. Some people will never get what you do, and will think you are messing up the neighbourhood. Others will nod with interest, but not get involved. And then there are those that think you are a genius.

Naturally, the more you can move people along the nature-friendly spectrum, the more natural the wider area may become. Maybe start a website or a page on your social media. Maybe put flyers up in the local community hall or on their website or socials. And post your story, your nature recovery journey, because stories always resonate with people, as we are social by design. Also share your wins and new stuff that turns up, since you are far more likely to change hearts and minds if you are seeing woodpeckers, owls and hedgehogs; results of your efforts.

If you are brave, give a talk to the local WI or community groups. Hold an event in your garden or on your patch; an open day, BBQ etc. If you need help, ask for volunteers. Maybe start a community group, a nature group, with regular talks, meet-ups or trips. If those trips are local walks to nearby good habitat or nature friendly spaces, then start a conversation within your group about the feasibility of creating a network between those patches. Invite the press or local council to support your efforts. Locals that are kindred spirits may be swayed to work on their own site. Common sense would suggest that your immediate neighbours are most important, because then you can directly connect to their land, allowing wildlife to flow into and out from your own plot. So if you can get them on board, talk about hedges, streams and other habitat continuity.

Finally start to think further afield. Maybe join or volunteer for the local Wildlife Trust, mammal group, or botany group for your county. (There are usually ones for birds (BTO or RSPB), bats, butterflies, reptiles and amphibians and even invertebrates usually too. They will usually have practical surveying work in the summer you can volunteer for, and interesting talks in the winter. It's a great way to make friends, contacts and to get out in nature. They may even come and do surveys on your plot for you if you ask them to, (usually for free, but they may be very busy in the relevant season).

And in a similar vein, if you are a larger site, talk to the staff at nearby nature reserves or schemes. They may be very interested in talking about how the sites can work together within the wider landscape, possibly even leading to a partnership. This is particularly true of Wildlife Trust sites or their Living Landscape areas, where it's not uncommon for them to mobilise their volunteers to help you manage your own site, particularly where it leads to shared goals, e.g. hedgerow improvement.

Fences, barriers and boundaries

Now we come on to a perennial thorn in nature's side - boundaries. Ever since Tudor times in the UK, we have enclosed common land to assign ownership to it. Unfortunately what is in place to keep your hens off the road, also prevents wildlife from roaming. And while a chaffinch may be unaffected by your garden wall, to a hedgehog it may as well be an eight lane highway.

So one of the prime actions as a landowner wanting to improve biodiversity on site is to remove all internal fences and to make all the boundary ones permeable. That is the optimal situation. Now wildlife can roam your site, and arrive, and leave, at will. However as I have alluded to before, it's not always that simple. The problems arise when you start to add livestock or domestic companions into the mix.

If you have dogs, you probably won't want holey boundaries that they can escape through, and therefore sadly, that foxes, badgers or deer can traverse. If you have chickens, geese, sheep or goats it will probably be the same. Cattle, donkeys and horses are probably still ok, even with young, and certainly you may get away with good hedges with larger stock.

It becomes a different problem if you have a common boundary with someone else that has dogs or stock. They may well put up fencing themselves that wrecks your plans. Well I guess to a point you would have to roll with it. You could see if they were sympathetic and could create a corridor from your boundary, across their land. If not, at least you have other boundaries where you may have more luck.

With your own stock, you may not want to remove all internal fencing, allowing maternity and quarantine or worming areas for livestock. Or you may want the option to graze the animals on rotation and require gates and fencing for that.

Other options in this scenario would be to use mobile electric fencing, which can change pasture areas within minutes. More recently no-fence collars have arrived that use a mild electric shock or audible alarm to remind domestic animals that they are at a boundary. Naturally boundaries are programmed into software, so there are no actual barriers on the ground. No-fence collars however, do need a large plot size, as the virtual boundary must presently be 150m from the actual boundary. Hopefully this will come down in time. Plus they aren't effective in all species. Additionally, I'm not entirely sure how tested they are in court, were your heifers to plough into the road regardless.

Sometimes you just have to be pragmatic, and zone your stock in one area, where larger wild mammals just won't tread. Obviously the effect of their herbivory driving mosaic habitats will likewise be limited to that zone however.

Step Five - chemicals

Stopping the use of chemicals on land, such as pesticides, fungicides, herbicides, and synthetic fertilisers, can greatly improve biodiversity in several ways:

- Chemicals can disrupt the natural balance of the soil, harming beneficial microbes and organisms that are essential for nutrient cycling and soil structure.
- Herbicides can reduce plant diversity - while targeting and eliminating specific species, they often affect non-target plants. Low variation in plants does not support a rich variety of wildlife.
- Pesticides harm or kill non-target species, particularly beneficial insects, then moving up the food chain to birds, bats and other small mammals. Pollinators such as bees and butterflies are particularly sensitive to pesticides, such as neonicotinoids.
- Chemicals often run off into water bodies, causing pollution that can harm aquatic life and disrupt ecosystems. Fertilisers are particularly damaging, causing algal growth that deoxygenates the water, killing other aquatic wildlife.

- All these chemicals result in a lack of biodiversity throughout the food web, so the resulting ecosystems are not resilient to environmental changes such as drought, disease, and pests.

So reducing chemical use:

- allows soil organisms to thrive, supporting healthier soil;
- more plant species will grow and flourish, providing varied habitats and food sources;
- wildlife populations can rebound, and species interactions can occur more naturally;
- supports the health and diversity of pollinators, which is crucial for the reproduction of many plants and overall ecosystem health;
- on land can improve water quality, supporting a diverse range of aquatic species;
- supports the development of a varied landscape that can better withstand and adapt to challenges and
- can help maintain or restore natural ecosystems, supporting a more diverse range of native species and their habitats.

I do realise that in saying, "stop using chemicals", many reading this from a development, farming or horticultural background will scornfully say "how?" And to a point, I understand the frustration. Going organic is not something that can be entered into lightly when it requires you to change your entire farming/horticultural set up. Plus there isn't always surety in the market, and certainly regenerative agriculture particularly requires a gradual transition of fields across the farm, over 5-10 years! So as I say I do understand something of the challenge. Development usually has more options by physically removing plants where required, and certainly has no excuse to landscape with chemicals. However, if I can play devil's advocate by reminding people that chemicals, inputs and diesel are never going to get cheaper, that controllable variable costs are called that for a reason, and as they will keep going up, your margins will always be going down. And since all the methods that rely on these chemicals reduce soil health, the only way to break out of the vicious circle is to do things differently. So plan a future where you are less reliant on the petrochemical markets, and where you know your costs in advance. Plenty are succeeding. Alternatives include organic farming practices, integrated pest management (such as wildflower margins and beetle banks, where there is evidence of increased yields over pesticides), and planting diverse crop rotations. Or cover cropping, intercropping, mintill or zerotill drilling, aftermath grazing etc. These methods promote a more natural balance and can lead to healthier and more sustainable ecosystems. They naturally require expert advice, some self education, and mentoring or support, however, that doesn't make them unattainable.

If you can't stop chemical applications, can you reduce them? Can you hire weather stations to minimise fungicide use (and cost). How uptodate is your tractor sat nav? You can usually programme them to within a few centimetres these days to minimise chemical spray drift (and save fuel). Plus if you put your mind to it, you can reduce soil compaction by programming the same course, and reduce it still further if all your axle widths are the same. How close to the ground are sprayers; again to minimise drift? Can you plant hedges or treelines to protect biodiverse areas and watercourses from drift and runoff. Wider field edge margins prevent you spraying too close to vulnerable areas. Ploughing and passing your vehicle tracks across the slope will minimise erosion and pollution runoff from hills. Minimising the annual number of passes you make will reduce soil compaction, so aiding water and chemical infiltration, (and again reduce fuel bills), as will keeping a root in the ground.

In gardens, ditch the glyphosate, the slug pellets and fertilisers (and use peat free compost - 1000 yrs to produce one metre of peat!). If you have room, chickens love slugs, and do fertilise as they go. Manure and chicken compost are excellent fertilisers for the veg and flower beds. However, don't forget your rewilding plot won't need fertilising if you want flowers rather than nettles.

Finally, another powerful group of agents that kill invertebrates, especially dung beetles, are livestock worming products, particularly ivermectins. Again not easy to do without, yet, also, many people are successfully achieving this and keeping their stock healthy. Options include reducing stocking levels so animals are less likely to graze near dung, short rotational grazing if you have the space, mixed species grazing as most parasites are species specific and introducing a variety of forage, especially taller swards as 80% of the eggs are found within 5cm of the ground. Another option is to quarantine animals after worming for a few days until they are no longer dunging out the drug, thereby concentrating the chemical into one area of the site. Obviously the health of your stock is paramount, so talk to other owners that are already practising these approaches and your vet before changing your animal health plan.

Step Six - people

Connectivity

Nature connectivity is at an all time low. With urban living becoming more and more the norm, people are becoming progressively further removed from nature. Now, not only is this a decided tragedy for those people, but it also makes it increasingly difficult to motivate people to act for nature, just when nature is most vulnerable, and by default, so are we. Nature provides us with every breath of oxygen, water, all our food, protection from floods, fires, droughts and storms, great physical and mental wellbeing, stable foundations to our financial markets and longer life. We cannot survive without nature, yet as a species we continue to be apathetic about curbing our lifestyles and allowing nature off the leash.

For people to champion nature, they need to love it. And to love it, they have to have a personal connection to it. And for that, they have to have access to it. And that is where you can come in. By including people to some degree in your project, you are helping create more nature lovers.

So how do you increase the impact of the uptick in wildlife on your site on people? Because for all the reasons above, rewilding is rooted in creating landscapes where nature and people thrive side by side, both urban and rural. We want people again to feel part of the natural world, for after all, we are just one of the myriad species on earth.

Roles

Well luckily there are many options, although naturally some are site size dependent:

- Firstly, you and your family (or colleagues if it is a work site) get to live amongst the glorious habitats, fauna and flora that you establish. You will find it a massive support for your mental health, and likely useful to your physical health. You'll start to notice birds, plants and bugs more than you did. You will start to feel a genuine connection to the land, as a proud custodian, and you will start to prioritise nature more in the rest of your life, many people find new purpose in life, and build friendships amongst the huge global family of nature lovers and restorers. To that end, start finding people to follow on social media. If you are just starting and want kindred spirits, you'll find thousands of nature lovers on Facebook and Instagram. However, if you want to immerse yourself in rewilding, I personally recommend LinkedIn, where all the organisations, professionals, influencers and people doing this for a living hang out - then you will truly come to realise how huge, positive and supportive the global nature recovery family is. It's the greatest antidote to ecoanxiety;

- If you are a large site, you may employ people. And those staff will get to spend their working hours surrounded by nature, feeling very uplifted by their job. And in turn, that is a wonderful opportunity that you have provided;
- Medium and large sites may well encourage volunteers, hopefully from the local community. Volunteers are always your greatest ambassadors, because they love what they do, and you are enriching their lives by giving them the chance. Plus that is a great way of giving back to your community. While we are on the subject, volunteering is a great way to get out in wonderful nature-rich spaces. So if you are reading this and thinking, "But I only have a window box!"; volunteer - it will do you the world of good. Great talks in winter, beautiful wildlife in summer, learn loads, make new friends, get fresh air, get active (the green gym) and become an expert on biscuits, trust me you will love it;
- Think about liaising with local schools - one site gifted each reception year child at the local village school one orchard tree, to care for with their family, pruning and fruit gathering, throughout their time at school, whilst giving them a bond to the site, and nature;
- Think of other ways to increase community engagement and connectivity - events,

- educational talks and community group activities;
- Do you have any footpaths or bridleways across the site? If not can you add some permissive paths (although signage, and potentially fencing may be necessary, and costly). Access is of increasing importance as people are estranged from the land and nature, so anything you can do to improve that, is always positive;
- If access is impractical, maybe you can post about your habitats, species and successes on your social media or create a website, thereby bringing your site into people's lives. Good nature photography always appeals, as it helps people destress and relax.

So my final nugget of advice to you, is to make a people plan, a manifesto of how you will use your wild home to make a difference from your community, and possibly beyond. If the neighbours kids grow up with more birdsong in their childhood, that they later think back to with nostalgia, you're winning. If a lonely retiree is healed by making friends among fellow volunteers at your place, then you've succeeded. And if you find you now love spending time sitting by the pond, with the wind rustling the willow leaves, and if you're maybe going on a bear spotting holiday in the Carpathians this Autumn, I think we can say job done!

Checklist

I thought it might be useful to create this checklist of what actions we have discussed in each section, so that you can tick off what you do. Don't worry, you don't have to do them all, in fact some would not always be appropriate. But do try to complete at least one action from each of the six steps to really help nature.

Step One - plants

Plant trees

Plant / repair hedges

Sow Meadows

Repair Soils

Step Two - animals

Support wild herbivores

Control wild herbivores

Domestic proxies

Herbivore mimicry

Reintroduce herbivores

Support wild predators

Support wild herbivores

Control wild herbivores

Domestic proxies

Herbivore mimicry

Reintroduce herbivores

Support wild predators

Control wild predators

Predator mimicry

Reintroduce predators

Support decomposers and scavengers

Support invertebrates

Animal disturbance mimicry

Step Three - water

Blocking or removing drains

Repairing existing riparian zones

Removing invasive species

Reintroducing aquatic species

Removing dams and weirs

Rewriggling and/or reprofiling streams

Creating leaky dams on streams

Increasing the complexity of floodplains

Create new ponds and scrapes

Step Four - Connections

Buy more land for nature

Create or improve onsite physical corridors

Create or improve onsite physical stepping stones - islands or headlands

Create or improve offsite physical corridors

Create or improve offsite physical stepping stones - islands or headlands

Set up a site website with your nature improvement journey

Set up social media pages for your site with your nature improvement journey

Talk to neighbours

Give talks to local groups

Hold an event / BBQ

Start a nature group or join a group

Volunteer with local organisations

Partner with local organisations

Make external boundaries more / less permeable

Remove internal barriers

Create internal barriers

Step Five - chemicals

Reduce or halt inorganic fertiliser use

Reduce or halt herbicide use

Reduce or halt pesticide use

Reduce or halt fungicide use

Go peat-free

Reduce, halt or mitigate wormer use

Step Six - people

People living on site amongst nature

People working on site amongst nature

People volunteering on site amongst nature

People have access to the site

Community are engaged with the site

Schools are engaged with the site

Create a website that engages people

Glossary

Introduction

Biomes: Large, distinct ecological areas characterised by specific climate, soil, and vegetation types.

Biodiversity: The variety of living organisms present in a particular ecosystem or habitat.

Community: A group of organisms living and interacting in a shared environment.

Decomposers: Organisms that break down organic matter into simpler substances, playing a crucial role in nutrient cycling.

Ecosystem: A community of living organisms interacting with each other and their environment.

Fauna: The animal species of a particular region or habitat.

Flora: The plant species of a particular region or habitat.

Herbivores: Animals that primarily feed on plants.

Nature hotspot: A location characterised by a high level of biodiversity and ecological significance.

Nature recovery: The process of restoring and revitalising natural ecosystems, often through conservation efforts, rewilding, and habitat restoration.

Planetary support system: The Earth's natural systems and processes that support life, including air, water, soil, and biodiversity.

Predators: Animals that hunt and feed on other animals.

Rewilding: A conservation approach that aims to restore ecosystems to their natural state by reintroducing native species, removing human interventions, and allowing natural processes to occur.

Self-sustainability: The ability of an ecosystem to maintain itself without significant external inputs or interventions.

Wellbeing: The state of being comfortable, healthy, and happy.

Step One - plants

Abundance: The number of individuals of a species present in a particular area. As you see below, biodiversity usually describes the variety of species present. So you could have lots of species, like in the UK, and therefore have fantastic biodiversity. But that's not the full story, because in the UK we have awful abundance - so we have lots of species, but not many individual animals, so many are in danger of going extinct! So both biodiversity and abundance are important.

Bare earth scrapes: Areas of exposed soil or ground, typically created by natural or human disturbance.

Biodiversity: The variety of life forms present in a particular habitat, ecosystem or biome. It can describe the variety of species, the variety of ecosystems, or even the variety of genes present.

Canopy: The upper layer of foliage in a forest or woodland, formed by the crowns of the tallest trees.

Carbon sequestration: The capture and storage of carbon dioxide from the atmosphere, often by plants and soil.

Coppicing: Cutting trees or shrubs to ground level to encourage new growth from the remaining "stool'.

Corridors: Routes through the landscape that facilitate movement for wildlife.

Dead hedging: Creating barriers using dead branches or brushwood.

Diversity: The variety of different species within an ecosystem - how "species rich" it is

Germination: The process by which a seed begins to grow and develop into a new plant.

Grazing: The act of feeding on grass or other vegetation, typically done by herbivorous animals.

Grasses: Herbaceous plants with narrow leaves, typically forming the predominant vegetation in meadows. They grow from the base of the plant to protect them from grazing.

Habitat: The natural environment where a particular species lives.

Hedge laying: The process of rejuvenating or restoring hedgerows through virtually cutting through vertical stems, staking them down horizontally and allowing them to regrow vertical stems from these.

Hedgerows: Rows of shrubs or trees, often used to divide or enclose fields or property.

Herbivory: The consumption of plant material by animals, often referred to as grazing or browsing by herbivores.

Invasive species: Non-native species that can spread rapidly, outcompeting native species, disrupting ecosystems, or spreading diseases. Examples include grey squirrels, american mink, snowberry, himalayan balsam and rhododendron in the UK.

Margins: The boundary or edge of a habitat, often characterised by unique plant communities. Normally used to refer to the edge of agricultural fields or ponds.

Mimicry: The imitation or replication of natural processes or features within an ecosystem.

Mycorrhizal network: The web of millions of fungal strands (hyphae) that form a symbiotic association with the roots of plants, facilitating nutrient uptake and exchange.

Native plants: Species that naturally occur and have evolved in a specific region or habitat.

Niches: The specific roles or functions that different species play within an ecosystem.

Pest control: The management or reduction of pest populations, often through natural predators or ecological processes.

Pollination: The transfer of pollen from one flower to another, facilitating fertilisation and reproduction.

Pollinators: Animals such as bees, butterflies, and birds that transfer pollen between flowers

Provenance: The original source or geographical location of a particular plant or seed.

Restoration projects: Efforts to rehabilitate or revive degraded ecosystems or habitats.

Riparian corridors: Strips of vegetation along riverbanks, streams or ponds, that form areas of transition between terrestrial and aquatic ecosystems.

Ruderal: dominant, often taller, dare I say, weed species, like nettles, docks and thistles. Usually the colonisers of waste ground.

Runoff: The movement of contaminants and pollutants from land surfaces into water bodies, often via rainfall or irrigation.

Seed banks: Deposits of seeds in the soil, capable of germinating under suitable conditions.

Soil stabilisation: Methods of preventing soil erosion or degradation.

Structural variation: Differences in the physical arrangement or composition of a habitat, such as varied tree heights or ages.

Variation: Differences or diversity within a population or ecosystem.

Water management: The control or regulation of water resources to minimise flooding or drought.

Step Two - animals

Agroforestry: A land use system that integrates trees and shrubs with crops and/or livestock in a harmonious manner.

Arthropods: The most diverse group of invertebrates, or animals on the planet, characterised by their segmented bodies, 6 jointed limbs, and an exoskeleton

Auditory Deterrents: Sound-based stimuli used to deter animals from certain areas, often involving recordings of predator calls or loud noises that often sound like guns

Bare Earth: Exposed soil or substrate without vegetation cover, important for certain insect and bird species, caused by disturbance like landslides or from pigs, and an important part of habitat diversity

Biosecurity: Measures taken to prevent the spread of infectious diseases or pests among livestock, crops, and wildlife.

Carrion: Dead and decaying flesh, typically referring to the remains of dead animals.

Coppice: A traditional method of woodland management involving cutting trees to ground level to promote the growth of new shoots.

Deadwood: Fallen or standing dead trees and branches, important for biodiversity as habitat for birds, bats, and for invertebrates as both that, and as a source of nutrients.

Disturbance: Events or processes that disrupt the structure or composition of an ecosystem, often leading to ecological succession.

Ecological Networks: Interconnected systems of species interactions and ecological processes within an ecosystem. A bit like food webs, but for all the other interactions between creatures too, like competition, pollination, parasitism, symbiotic relationships etc.

Feasibility Studies: Investigations conducted to determine the practicality and viability of conservation projects or reintroducing a species into a specific ecosystem.

Grazing: The act of feeding on grass or other vegetation, typically done by herbivorous animals.

Habitat Creation: The establishment or restoration of suitable habitats to support native species, often through habitat enhancement measures.

Habitat Enhancement: The improvement or restoration of natural habitats to support native wildlife populations.

Habitat Management: The deliberate manipulation of habitats to achieve specific conservation or ecological goals.

Herbivores: Animals that primarily feed on plants.

Invertebrates: Animals without a backbone, including insects, spiders, crustaceans, and mollusks.

Landscape of Fear: The concept describing how the presence of predators influences the behaviour and distribution of prey species within an ecosystem.

Meadows: Open grassland habitats characterised by diverse plant species, often containing wildflowers and grasses.

Mega Herbivores: Large herbivorous animals that play significant roles in shaping ecosystems, like bison, horses and cows. In times past they would have included elephants, rhino and giant ground sloths.

Microhabitat: literally habitat at really small scale. So we might deem a habitat to be a hedgerow, while microhabitat could be a small tussocky patch of grass

Mimicry: The imitation of natural processes or ecological roles through human intervention to achieve similar outcomes. A lot more work than nature doing it, however, a good compromise in some situations

Mitigation Techniques: Strategies employed to minimise or offset the negative impacts of human activities (usually) on the environment or wildlife.

Native Breeds: Animal breeds that are indigenous to a particular region and have adapted to the local environment over time. E.g. exmoor ponies

Necrobiome: The community of organisms involved in the decomposition of dead organisms and organic matter in the environment.

Omnivore: An animal that consumes both plants and animals as part of its diet.

Plant Succession: The process by which plant communities change over time in a particular area due to competition, colonisation, and environmental factors.

Predator: An animal that preys on other organisms for food such as a weasel.

Proxy Species: Substitutes for extinct or absent species that perform similar ecological functions.

Raptors: Birds of prey, including eagles, hawks, falcons, and owls, known for their predatory behaviour.

Reintroduction: The deliberate release of a species back into its native ecosystem after extinction, local or national, often aimed at restoring ecological balance, and filling a missing niche.

Rewilding: The process of restoring or reintroducing natural processes and species to an ecosystem, often with some initial kick-start actions aimed at renewing ecological resilience, to promote biodiversity, abundance and ecological balance.

Rootle: The action of pigs and boar turning over soil and whatever is growing on it, as they hunt for grubs, worms and tubers.

Stocking Level: The number of animals grazing on a given area of land

Supplementary Feeding: Providing additional food to livestock, usually given when the grazing and foraging available are inadequate for them to stay in good condition.

Sward: An expanse of grass, pasture or meadow

Veteran Trees: Old trees of significant age and ecological importance, often providing habitat for numerous species.

Visual Deterrents: Objects or stimuli designed to deter animals from specific areas through visual cues, such as model animals, kites or scarecrows.

Wood Pasture: A habitat that combines elements of both woodland and grassland, characterised by scattered trees or small copses within a grazed meadow. Perhaps exemplified by British parkland and Spanish dehesa.

Step Three - water

Clay Liners: Impermeable barriers made of clay or clay-based materials used to prevent water seepage or leakage in ponds, landfills, and other structures.

Extirpated: Locally extinct; no longer present in a specific area, though still existing elsewhere.

Floodplains: Low-lying areas adjacent to rivers or streams that are prone to flooding during periods of high water flow.

Groundwater Recharge: The process by which water from precipitation or surface water sources infiltrates into the soil and replenishes underground aquifers.

Hydrology: The study of water and its movement, distribution, and properties on Earth, including its effects on the environment and human society.

Leaky Dams: Low structures built across streams or rivers designed to temporarily impound water, allowing sediment to settle and creating habitats for aquatic species.

Oxbows: U-shaped bends or curves in a river formed when a meander is cut off from the main channel, creating a still or slow-moving body of water.

Pollutants: Harmful substances or contaminants introduced into the environment, often through human activities, that can have adverse effects on ecosystems and human health.

Reservoirs: Artificial or natural bodies of water used for storing water, regulating stream flow, and generating hydropower.

Structural Complexity: The degree of variation and diversity in physical features within an ecosystem, such as the shape and composition of habitats.

Terrestrial: Relating to or occurring on land, as opposed to aquatic or marine environments.

Topography: The physical features of the land surface, including its elevation, slope, and relief.

Step Four - connections

Boundaries: Physical or conceptual lines that separate one area from another, such as property lines, walls, fences, hedges, or natural features.

Connectivity: The degree to which landscapes or habitats are connected or interconnected, facilitating the movement of organisms and genetic exchange between populations.

Core Habitat: Areas with high-quality, undisturbed habitat that support thriving populations of native species. Some species thrive in core habitat, but may not behave normally (e.g. feeding and breeding) in edge habitat, such as corridors and some stepping stones. Some species prefer the edges instead.

Corridors: Linear features such as hedgerows, streams, or forest edges that provide pathways for wildlife movement between patches of habitat.

Domestic Animals: Livestock or pets that are kept by humans for companionship, work, or producing food or materials like wool, leather or horn.

Electric Fencing: A type of fencing that delivers an electric shock to deter animals from crossing a boundary.

Habitat Fragmentation: The breaking up of natural habitats into smaller, isolated patches, often due to human activities such as urbanisation, agriculture, or infrastructure development.

Patch Size: The area of a habitat or ecosystem, often used in ecological studies to analyse the effects of habitat fragmentation on species diversity and abundance.

Permeable Fencing: Fences or barriers that allow the passage of wildlife while still providing some level of containment for domestic animals. E.g. you could remove a few stones to create a tunnel through a dry-stone wall.

Quarantine Areas: Designated spaces used to isolate and monitor animals suspected of carrying infectious diseases or parasites, often used in livestock management.

Saproxylic Beetles: Insects that depend on dead or decaying wood for some part of their life cycle, often associated with deadwood, old-growth forests and veteran trees.

Stepping Stones: Small patches of habitat dispersed throughout a landscape that serve as refuges or stopover sites for wildlife moving between larger core areas.

Step Five - chemicals

Aftermath Grazing: Allowing livestock to graze on crop residues, such as stubble, after harvest, promoting nutrient cycling, soil health, and animal nutrition.

Cover Cropping: The practice of growing crops, often non-harvested, to cover and protect the soil between main crops, enhancing soil fertility, moisture retention, and biodiversity.

Ecosystem Resilience: The ability of an ecosystem to resist and recover from disturbances, such as drought, disease, or human activities.

Fungicides: Chemical substances used to kill or inhibit the growth of fungi that cause plant diseases.

Glyphosate: A broad-spectrum herbicide widely used to kill weeds and unwanted plants.

Herbicides: Chemical substances used to kill or control unwanted plants or weeds.

Integrated Pest Management (IPM): A holistic approach to pest control that combines biological, cultural, physical, and chemical methods to minimise economic, health, and environmental risks.

Inter-cropping: Growing two or more crops together in the same field at the same time, providing mutual benefits such as pest control, soil improvement, and resource use efficiency. E.g. If one crop requires more nitrogen and one prefers more phosphorus, they make better companions in the same space than two crops that both need lots of nitrogen.

Mintill or Zerotill Drilling: Techniques for planting crops without prior tillage or minimal soil disturbance, reducing erosion, preserving soil structure, and conserving moisture.

Neonicotinoids: A class of systemic insecticides that are chemically similar to nicotine and have been implicated in the decline of bee populations.

Non-Target Species: Organisms unintentionally affected by the application of pesticides or other chemicals.

Nutrient Cycling: The movement and exchange of nutrients between living organisms and their environment, including the soil, plants, and decomposers.

Organic Farming: A method of agricultural production that avoids the use of synthetic chemicals, pesticides, and fertilisers, focusing on natural processes and biodiversity conservation.

Peat: A valuable and slow-renewing resource extracted from wetlands.

Peat-free Compost: Compost or soil mixtures that do not contain peat, a valuable and slow-renewing resource extracted from wetlands.

Pesticides: Chemical substances used to kill or control pests such as insects, weeds, and fungi.

Soil Structure: The arrangement and organisation of soil particles, pores, and aggregates, which influence water infiltration, root penetration, and nutrient availability.

Synthetic (or inorganic) Fertilisers: Chemical substances containing essential nutrients such as nitrogen, phosphorus, and potassium, used to promote plant growth and productivity. As opposed to organic fertilisers such as compost, or farmyard manure (FYM).

Step Six - people

Ambassadors: People who represent and promote a particular organisation, cause, or idea, often by sharing their experiences and advocating for its goals.

Community Engagement: The process of involving and interacting with community members to address local issues, promote participation, and build relationships.

Custodian: Someone who has the responsibility for taking care of something, such as the land, and ensuring its well-being for future generations.

Eco-anxiety: A psychological condition characterised by feelings of stress, anxiety, or despair related to environmental issues, such as climate change or biodiversity loss.

Manifesto: A public declaration or statement of intentions, principles, or policies, often outlining goals and objectives for a specific cause or movement.

Nature Connectivity: The degree to which natural habitats are connected, allowing for the movement of species and ecological processes across landscapes.

Permissive Paths: Paths or routes that landowners, with their discretion, allow the public to use for recreational purposes, often with specific conditions or restrictions. (I.e. they are not Public Rights of Way which are a legal designation, from which the user has published rights)

Urban Living: A lifestyle characterised by living in cities or urban areas, often associated with high population density, infrastructure development, and limited access to natural environments.

Volunteers: Individuals who offer their time and services for free to support an organisation, cause, or project.

Acknowledgements

Thanks to my LinkedIn family of friends that provide hope and inspiration daily. And to the rest of the rewilders, ecologists, landowners and managers that I hang out with, for being the friendliest and most helpful bunch of people ever.

And finally...

For more - much, much more, of the why and the how, get in touch with me at my company, A Call to ReWild, via the website contact page at www.acalltorewild.co.uk

We have courses and programmes for interested individuals, home and landowners wanting to give back, and land businesses that want to increase turnover or qualify for subsidies without negatively impacting on their present operation.

Printed in Great Britain
by Amazon